From Cuneiform to COMPUTERS

D1487527

Mark McArthur-Christie

OXFORD
UNIVERSITY PRESS

OXFORD
UNIVERSITY PRESS

Great Clarendon Street, Oxford OX2 6DP

Oxford University Press is a department of the University of Oxford.
It furthers the University's objective of excellence in research, scholarship,
and education by publishing worldwide in

Oxford New York

Athens Auckland Bangkok Bogotá Buenos Aires Cape Town Chennai
Dar es Salaam Delhi Florence Hong Kong Istanbul Karachi Kolkata
Kuala Lumpur Madrid Melbourne Mexico City Mumbai Nairobi
Paris São Paulo Shanghai Singapore Taipei Tokyo Toronto Warsaw

with associated companies in Berlin Ibadan

Oxford is a registered trade mark of Oxford University Press
in the UK and in certain other countries

Published in the United Kingdom by Oxford University Press

British Library Cataloguing in Publication Data

Data available

ISBN 0 19 917442 3

Also available in packs
Communications Inspection Pack (one of each book) ISBN 0 19 917446 6
From Cuneiform to Computers Guided Reading Pack (six copies) ISBN 0 19 917860 7
Communications Class Pack (six of each book) ISBN 0 19 917447 4

www.oup.com/uk/primary

Printed in Hong Kong

Acknowledgements

The Publisher would like to thank the following for permission to reproduce photographs:
p 4 Mary Evans Picture Library; p 5 Science & Society Picture Library (top), Shout Picture Agency (bottom); p 6 Ancient Art
& Architecture; p 7 Pitt Rivers Museum; p 8 Ancient Art & Architecture (bottom left); p 9 Mary Evans Picture Library (top),
Ms 540 f.3r Page with historiated initial 'M' depicting St. Andrew, from a choir book from San Marco e Cenacoli (vellum) by
Domenico Ghirlandaio (Domenico Bigordi) (1449–94) Museo di San Marco dell'Angelico, Florence, Italy/Bridgeman Art
Library (centre right); pp 10, 12 Mary Evans Picture Library (all); p 13 Butler & Tanner (centre); p 14 Corbis UK (all);
p 15 Ancient Art & Architecture (top left and bottom), Corbis UK (right); p 16 Science & Society Picture Library; p 17 Science
& Society Picture Library (top), Corbis UK (bottom); p 18 Marconi plc (top), Science & Society Picture Library (bottom left);
p 19 Hulton Getty (top), Mary Evans Picture Library (right), Corbis UK (bottom); p 20 Science & Society Picture Library;
p 21 Science Photo Library/F Sauze; p 22 Mary Evans Picture Library (top), Hulton Getty (bottom); p 23 Mary Evans Picture
Library (top), Hulton Getty (bottom left), Shout Picture Library (bottom right); p 24 Science & Society Picture Library (centre
& left), Shout Picture Library (top), Science Photo Library/D Martin (bottom), /C Falco (left); p 28 Shout Picture Library.

Front cover photograph by Ancient Art & Architecture
Back Cover by Mary Evans Picture Library

Illustrated by Martin Aston, Kathy Baxendale, Stefan Chabluk, John Holder and James Sneddon

Despite every effort to trace copyright holders, this has not been possible in every case.
If notified, the publisher will be pleased to rectify any omissions at the earliest opportunity.

Contents

What is Communication?

When people make contact with each other and send messages, we say they "communicate" with each other. They write letters with pens or word processors, use computers to send e-mails, and talk on the telephone. They watch programmes on the TV and listen to the radio. All these things were invented by someone!

▲ A monk writing a manuscript

The four ages of communication

This book is about communication and the communication inventions that changed the world. It divides the history of communication into four ages:

THE MANUAL AGE 5 BC – AD 1454

In the Manual Age, when people wanted to send information over long distances, they had to write it down. Some civilizations did not have a system of writing and so communicated in different ways.

> **DID YOU KNOW?**
>
> **Old words today**
> The word "manual" comes from the Latin word "manus" for hand.

THE MECHANICAL AGE

1455 – 1837
This began with the invention of printing and newspapers. People used printing machines to help them communicate with more people and more quickly.

◀ William Caxton, in 1474, demonstrating his new printing press to King Edward IV in London.

THE ELECTRIC AGE 1838 – 1937

By using electricity the telegraph, the telephone and early radios and televisions meant people could communicate using sound, as well as pictures, over long distances.

A Morse key ▶

THE ELECTRONIC AGE 1937 – TODAY

Satellites, computers, the Internet and e-mail allow you to communicate with people, almost instantly, all over the world.

▲ The computer has become an important communication tool.

HOW DOES COMMUNICATION WORK?

Communication needs two or more people to make it work; a sender and a receiver. Successful communication depends on the sender making the message clear and the receiver understanding it.

▲ You can see clearly what this policeman wants you to do, even though you cannot hear him.

You communicate nearly all the time – sometimes even when you don't know it. You communicate aloud when you speak, when you laugh and when you shout. And you can do it silently too, when you smile or frown. Even what you wear communicates something about you.

The Manual Age

Marks on paper

When you write, you make marks on paper that someone else can interpret.

Writing is very important in our society. When you were born, your parents had to have an official birth certificate written out with your name on it and theirs. When you sit in lessons in school your teachers will give you information by writing on the board. Everywhere you look there is writing.

◄ Some of the first writing used pictures for words instead of separate letters. In cuneiform writing, the word for barley looked like a simple stem of barley (top). Later it looked more elaborate (middle). Later still, the words were turned on their sides (bottom).

◄ A cuneiform clay tablet showing stylus indentations

Cuneiform means "wedge-shaped".

Cuneiform writing was used in the Middle East, about 3000 years ago. The tool used for cuneiform writing was a special pointed stick, called a **stylus**, which was pressed into a flat piece of clay. Then the clay was baked to make it hard.

When letters represent things, like the cuneiform word for barley, they are called **ideograms**.

But it is hard to write about complicated subjects and ideas using ideograms, so a new way of writing evolved, called syllabic writing, where the written symbols were groups of letters, or **syllables**. This example is in the Hindi language, written in Devanagari script.

A Hindu ► poem written in Devanagari script

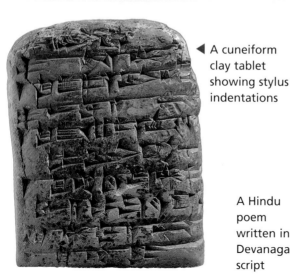

तन्हाँ है ज़िन्दगी

तन्हां है दस कदर अव ज़िन्दगी
की स्वपन भी कतराने लगे
दुनियाँ से हुये दूर हम,
आँसु ही मन भाने लगे

The Ancient Greeks took the idea of syllabic writing a stage further, creating individual letters to stand for the sounds we call **vowels** and **consonants**. Our modern alphabet has its origins in the Greek and Roman alphabets.

The Inca people, who ruled in South America more than 14,000 years ago, did not have a system of writing. Even without it they had one of the largest empires of the ancient world. To organize their trade, **taxes** and armies they recorded very complex mathematics by using knotted pieces of coloured string to make a patterned net called a **quipu**.

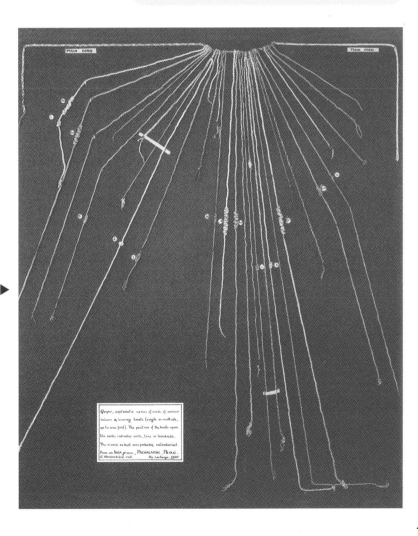

In an Inca quipu, each colour, ▶ knot, space and pattern stood for a different set of numbers.

Writing through the Ages

Scribes to scriptoria

In many ancient civilizations most people could not read or write: they were **illiterate**. A few people, called scribes, were trained to read and write for the whole community. The scribes often became rich and powerful because they could control business and politics.

A pharaoh **dictating** ▶ a message for a scribe to write down

The Ancient Greek civilization was the first in which nearly every citizen could read and write. They thought anyone who did not speak Greek could not possibly be civilized.

> ### DID YOU KNOW?
>
> In Ancient Egyptian **hieroglyphic** writing, you can see that the word for "scribe" was made up from the things he used to write: a bag full of reed pens, an ink bag and a palette for mixing the ink.
>
>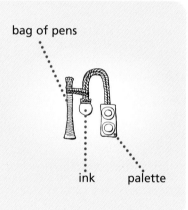
>
> bag of pens
>
> ink   palette

The Greeks called them "barbarians" (or *barbaroi* in Greek), because they made a noise sounding like "bar bar bar bar" when they spoke.

Most Roman citizens could read and write. The Roman alphabet was adapted from the Greek alphabet. It looked like the alphabet most people in Western countries write with today.

◀ An inscription written in the Roman alphabet

When the Roman empire collapsed, around AD 500, illiteracy became widespread. Even many kings and chiefs could not read; they were too busy fighting! During these times, the writing was done in monasteries where monks wrote in rooms, called "scriptoria". The rooms had lots of windows to make them light. The monks copied books out by hand, often adding beautiful drawings and decorations. These are called illuminated manuscripts.

It took many months to write a book like this, and the monks did it to show their devotion to God. The writing they use is sometimes called "black letter gothic". Red ink was used to highlight important words and the names of saints. This is where we get the expression "red letter day", because the days when saints' lives were celebrated were sometimes holidays or festival days.

Now that nearly all important information is ▶ written down, everyone needs to be able to read and write.

Paper, Ink and Pens

The oldest writing that has been discovered, dating from 4000 BC, was cut into stone or clay tablets, making it heavy to carry and hard to store. The first type of "paper" was **papyrus.** The papery sheets were made from thin strips of plant material. It was used by the Egyptians who wrote on it with ink and reed pens, around 3500 BC.

▼ An Egyptian scribe writing on papyrus

▲ This 14th-century German papermill was operated by Italian workers who knew the secret of papermaking.

The first Chinese paper was invented about AD 105. It was made from rags, the bark of trees and old fishing nets!

Because people could only write by hand, which took a long time, there was no need for paper to be made in large quantities. When printing began in 1455, large amounts of paper were needed to produce hundreds of books. Paper mills were set up to supply the printing presses with paper.

Paper today is made from wood pulp from renewable forests.

Pens

Over 5000 years ago, Egyptians made pens from hollow reeds to write on papyrus. If you dip a narrow tube, such as a straw, in liquid, the liquid rises up the tube to form a small **reservoir**. With a coloured liquid, such as ink, in the tube, and a point at the end, you can make marks or write with your "pen".

▲ The stiff "quills" in large bird feathers were used as pens.

Ink

Until the 1880s, pens had to be dipped in the ink-well over and over again.

▲ A dipping pen

If the ink was too thick, it blocked the pen and stopped it writing. If it was too thin, it leaked and dripped everywhere. In 1884, a successful "reservoir pen" was invented, which held a tube of ink in a barrel behind the pen nib. We use the same basic design of "fountain pen" today.

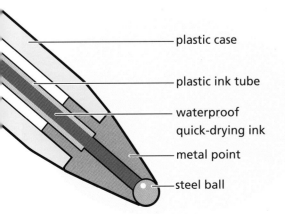

▲ An early fountain pen

plastic case

plastic ink tube

waterproof quick-drying ink

metal point

steel ball

Biros

In 1938, two Hungarian brothers, Ladislao and Georg Biro, made a pen that not only carried its ink with it, but did not leak and never needed filling. They gave their name to the ballpoint pen – the biro. The ink was made with fine oil which flowed out over a tiny rolling ball at the tip of the pen.

The Mechanical Age

Printing

Some inventions happen when someone takes things that have already been discovered and puts them together in a new way. This is how printing was re-invented in Europe.

Printing had been used in China since the 9th century. But the Chinese language has a symbol for each word, so printers needed thousands of printing blocks. It took a long time to print a book by hand so they were very expensive.

See Ideograms page 6

Words for everyone

In 1454, Johannes Gütenberg put together a wine press, a new kind of ink, paper and movable **type**, or letters. He arranged the individual letters of the alphabet into words and fixed them in a frame, coated them with ink and pressed them onto paper. Because he used separate letters to make the words, they could be rearranged and re-used so he was able to print books quickly and easily. Soon, books became more plentiful, and cheaper, so more people could afford them.

The first book Gütenberg printed was a bible. ▶ It cost 30 florins – more money than most people earned in three years!

DID YOU KNOW?

What is printing?
Words and pictures were printed by spreading ink onto a block and pressing it onto a piece of paper.

▲ The type on the block is a mirror image of the printed letter.

How Gütenberg made his printing blocks

Before Gütenberg, printing blocks had been made from wood. These took a long time to carve, and, because the wood was soft, the blocks wore out quickly.

Gütenberg invented a way of "casting" the letters ▶ made from lead, in copper moulds. Some special type was still cast by hand in the early 20th century.

▲ In modern printing huge machines can print thousands of pages in an hour. Pages of words and pictures are marked, or **engraved**, onto enormous steel rollers and the paper runs between them.

In 1884, a new method was developed for quickly casting whole lines of words in lead. This was called Linotype. Because the lines could be melted down and used again it meant that printing became even faster and cheaper. Ideas could spread faster than ever before.

Printing with a little separate block for each letter is called *Monotype*. Printing with whole lines of words is called *Linotype*.

Spreading the Word

Books and newspapers

Books are an important way of communicating ideas and thoughts. Books are powerful and valuable, and some books have changed the world. In Germany, in the early 1500s, Martin Luther's religious theories were published in books that made people all over Europe ask new questions about God. This eventually led to the church losing a lot of its power.

What were the first books like?

The first books were very different from books today. Many were hand-written on rolls of animal skin called **parchment** or **vellum**.

By the 7th century, monks were producing books that we would recognize. These had pages fastened

▲ A portrait of Martin Luther with a book of his **sermons**

together at the spine and a strong leather cover. The words and pictures were written and drawn at the same time, by hand. The first letters of paragraphs were filled with beautiful decorations. These are called "illuminated" letters.

These books were so valuable that they were often chained up to stop people stealing them. These books were mostly about religion. They were bibles, or books of prayers. The monks believed that by making them so beautifully they were worshipping God.

▲ A piece of ancient vellum manuscript

▲ This beautiful illuminated manuscript, *The Book of Kells,* was written by monks in the time of St Columba, who died in AD 597.

Movable type

By the 15th century, books printed with movable type became widespread. As well as religious books, there were books about new discoveries in science, medicine, astronomy and philosophy. Printing meant that many copies of the same book could be made, so ideas could travel fast.

See page 12

▲ The astronomer Copernicus wrote a book which challenged the idea that the Sun went round the Earth. It changed the way people thought about the Universe.

The first newspapers

The Romans had two sorts of newspapers: called *Acta Senatus* and *Acta Diurna.* The *Acta Senatus* was about things the Roman Senate, or government, had decided. It was only read by people in government. The *Acta Diurna* was read by many ordinary people and told them what the Senate had decided and how it would affect their lives.

◀ A chained book in Hereford Cathedral library

The Electric Age

Electricity and the new spark in communications

Before the invention of the telegraph, it was difficult to send messages over long distances. In 1791, a Frenchman, Claude Chappé, invented a mechanical **semaphore** signalling system. It had adjustable wooden crosses which moved to stand for different letters of the alphabet. But people could only send semaphore messages as far as they could see. Communicating over longer distances still relied on a messenger carrying a written message on horseback or on foot, which took a long time.

▲ A dispatch rider carried messages, or dispatches, on horseback.

In 1837, two British inventors, William Fothergill Cooke (1806 – 1879) and Charles Wheatstone (1802 – 1875) invented the telegraph.

An operator used iron needles to indicate letters and numbers on a wooden board, connected, by wires, to an identical board a long way off. The needles were moved by electricity and spelled out the message. The telegraph was used to send messages between railway stations. Wheatstone also invented the concertina in 1829!

◄ Cooke and Wheatstone's five-needle telegraph machine

Morse Code

In 1837, Samuel Morse, with help from his partner Alfred Vail, invented a system which sent electrical impulses along a wire over long distances. Morse invented a code with the letters of the alphabet represented by dots and dashes. Short and long impulses were used to signal the dots and dashes. Telegraph lines made it possible to send Morse Code messages a long way.

A German inventor made it possible to send two messages at the same time on the same wire. Later, an American, Thomas Edison found a way to send four messages at the same time! The messages were still in Morse Code and so they had to be de-coded.

Telegrams and teleprinters

In 1903, a Scot, Donald Murray, invented a way of printing letters rather than just the Morse Code symbols. This was used to send telegrams to post offices. Boys on bicycles delivered the telegrams to people's houses or businesses. By the 1930s, teleprinters using a similar system could print 500 letters or numbers an hour! Now people could send written messages from one country to another, as easily as writing a letter, but much more quickly than by using the postal system.

The message in Morse Code, ▶ printed on this long tape, was sent to a ship in the middle of the Atlantic while it was laying the cable under the ocean.

▲ A Morse Code recording machine with a tape drum

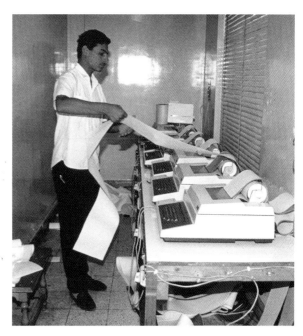

▲ A telex machine – a modern teleprinter

Radio – Messages without Wires

One of the major problems with the telegraph was that it needed wires. This meant you could only send or receive a written message at a **telegraph station** where there was a telegraph machine. If the wires were broken or cut, no one could send messages.

In 1888, a German inventor, Heinrich Hertz, showed that it was possible to transmit electricity through the air. The race to use radio waves had begun!

The first radio signals were sent by Guglielmo Marconi in 1894. By 1901, he was able to send a message in Morse Code from Cornwall to Newfoundland hundreds of kilometres across the Atlantic Ocean. People no longer had to rely on expensive and fragile cables laid under the sea to send messages.

In 1906, a Canadian engineer called Reginald Fessenden made a

▼ Guglielmo Marconi with his radio transmitter

breakthrough. He sent a message in speech more than 150 kilometres without using wires. He called his new invention "radio". By 1920, regular public radio broadcasts were made in the USA. People listened on "crystal sets" they made from kits. These radios had no loudspeakers so people listened through earphones.

▲ An old crystal set   A modern crystal set ▶

▼ You can still buy a crystal set kit to build a crystal radio (below) that will work in the same way as the old crystal set on the left.

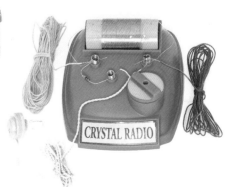

◄ The whole family used to gather round the "wireless" to listen to the news.

When King Edward VIII gave up the throne ► in 1936 he made a live broadcast to the British nation on the radio.

Now people could hear speech on their radios, governments could pass on important information quickly. The new technology also meant people could listen to the radio for entertainment. The invention of the electronic "valve" and other new technology made it possible to send signals even further.

▼ Many people now use pocket-size transistor radios with earphones.

The valves in early radios made the very faint signals they received sound louder. Because the valves only worked efficiently when they got hot, old radio sets had to be switched on to "warm up" before they would work.

By the 1960s, valves were replaced by much smaller "transistors". A transistor radio gives a much clearer sound than an old valve radio.

We now have **digital radio** with high-quality signals that can be sent across huge distances.

Television

With radio, speech and music could now be **transmitted**, or sent, using radio waves, but what about pictures?

Inventors realized that they could not send whole pictures using radio waves, but they thought it might be possible to send small pieces of a picture. In 1884, a German, Paul Nipkow, used a spinning disc with slots cut in it which cut up and re-assembled an image on a paper screen. The first real television images were made by a Russian, Boris Rosing. Rosing used Nipkow's spinning disk to display an image on the screen of a **cathode ray tube**. This sort of tube is used in most modern TV sets.

▼ The Maltese Cross

How a Maltese Cross changed the world for ever

In 1923, John Logie Baird used a machine with spinning discs to transmit a picture of a Maltese Cross from one room to another. This was the

▼ The equipment used for Baird's first television transmission

first time a television signal had been sent over any distance. Three years later he demonstrated the first, flickering TV transmission to an audience. In 1929, the first TV studio was opened in London by the BBC. Meanwhile, in the USA, the Russian, Vladimir Zworykin had invented an electronic TV camera and spinning discs were no longer needed.

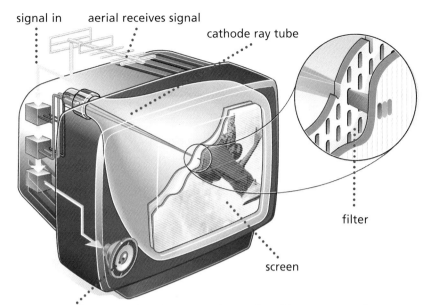

signal in   aerial receives signal

cathode ray tube

filter

screen

speaker

▲ A TV set receives a signal from a transmitter and it is converted into a picture on the screen of a cathode ray tube.

▼ Coloured TV pictures are made up from thousands of little dots like these.

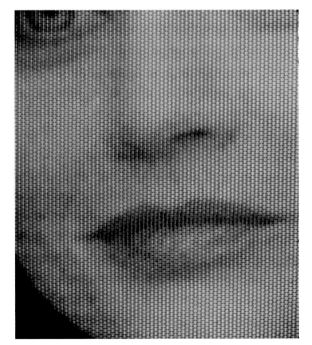

Television works by tricking your eye into thinking that you can see a whole image at once. In fact, the image on a TV screen is made up from 625 lines which each appear every twenty-fifth of a second, changing just faster than your eye can detect. This means that a moving picture on the screen seems to move smoothly.

Now, moving pictures and sound can be relayed from one country to another. All over the world people watched Neil Armstrong walk on the surface of the Moon in 1969. Now, news can be broadcast so fast that people can make up their own minds about national and international events as they watch, instead of reading reporters' opinions in the newspapers the next day.

The Telephone

On a telephone, you can talk to people a long way off – instantly! There is no need to write anything down, send a telegraph or use the dots and dashes of Morse Code. We can send news as soon as it happens for only a few pence. Using the phone, people in business can get information about things happening in other places far faster than they could when they had to rely on letters or messengers.

There are more than 500 million telephones in the world and, in the USA alone, more than two billion phone calls are made each day. We rely on the phone as a quick, easy, cheap and personal way of communicating.

Alexander Graham Bell was awarded a US patent for an early version of the telephone in 1876.

A metal-coated sheet in the mouthpiece of your phone converts the sounds into electrical "pulses". The signal travels along telephone wires to the person you are speaking to and is converted back into sounds in the earpiece of their phone.

◀ An early telephone

▼ Alexander Graham Bell sending the first telephone message from New York to Chicago

Old words today

The word "telephone" is made up from two Greek words, "tele" which means "far", and "phone" which means "sound". Originally it was the name for the speaking tubes that were common in large houses. People in different rooms could talk to each other using a tube with a cone at each end to **amplify** the sound.

Mobile phones use a similar method without involving wires. They turn speech into pulses that can be sent as radio waves to a local transmitter which then sends them on to a series of other transmitters across the country.

◀ A local transmitter for mobile phones

▼ Mobile phones can be used almost anywhere.

▲ Although telephones have changed a lot since they were invented by Bell, they still use the same basic principle.

23

The Electronic Age

Computers – clever counting machines

Today, computers are everywhere. This book has been written using a computerized word-processor. It makes writing much faster as all the rubbing out, changes and corrections can be done quickly on the screen. The design of the pages and some of the pictures have been created with a computer too.

The engine in a new car has a computer to constantly tune and control it. The car itself was designed by someone using a computer.

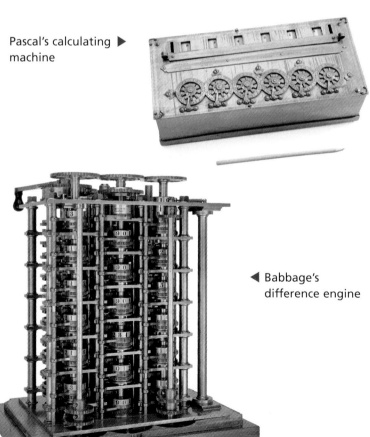

◀ Pascal's calculating machine

The first computers were mechanical. This adding machine was built by the French mathematician Blaise Pascal in 1642. It can add numbers from 1 to 999,999.

Charles Babbage, a British inventor, tried to build a more complicated computer which was **programmable** in 1823. He called it the "difference engine". Sadly, he never finished it, but he tried to make an even more complicated machine called the analytical engine in 1842, but again, never finished it.

◀ Babbage's difference engine

During the Second World War, a British mathematician, Alan Turing, worked out how to **decipher** the enemies' coded messages. He used a huge machine called the *Turing bombe* to do the calculations. In 1943, a much faster machine, called *Colossus*, was built and used for codebreaking. This was the first programmable electronic computer.

How do computers work?

Computers are "programmed" or made to work by reducing the information put in (the "input") to its simplest possible form. All the information is converted into a series of either "1s" or a "0s" in the form of pulses of electricity, with a 1 being a pulse and a 0 being no pulse.

The huge amounts of information in a computer are held on silicon chips. A single chip can hold as many as 450,000 electronic components.

Computers can do operations in seconds that used to take people years to complete. They have made many things easier for us as many of the hard, unpleasant jobs that used to be done by people are now done by computers.

▲ Alan Turing's work in mathematics led to the development of the modern computer.

▼ A car-assembly line with computerized robots

◀ A silicon chip on a finger

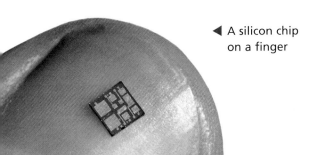

The Internet and the World Wide Web

A modern mine of information

Before printing was invented, information could only spread very slowly, by word of mouth, from person to person or by **laboriously** hand-copied manuscripts. Printing meant that information could be carried around easily in book form, and the world's libraries with thousands of books became huge stores of information. The World Wide Web on the Internet is like linking all those libraries together, adding even more information and making it all accessible from your computer.

▼ The World Wide Web links thousands of computers.

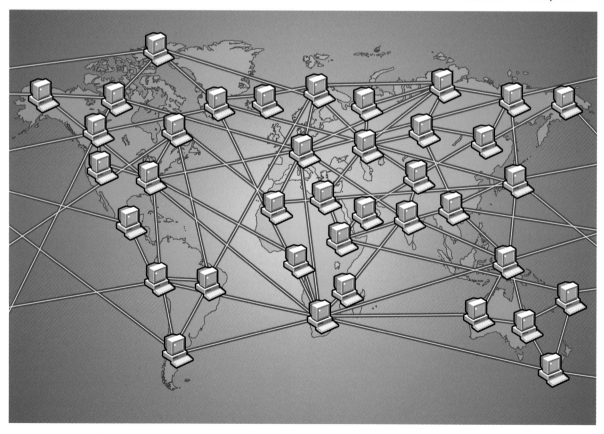

The Internet

The Internet began in 1969 when the US Department of Defense linked a series of computers together to form ARPANET, the Advanced Research Projects Agency Network. This enabled government researchers to see and share the same information quickly and securely.

Soon other researchers began to use the network, and the National Science Foundation created their own computer network. The Internet, as we know it, was born here, but soon spread across the world, and even into space!

The World Wide Web and e-mail

The most well-known parts of the Internet are the World Wide Web (or www) and e-mail. The web acts like a window which allows people to look at the information on the Internet. With e-mail you can send messages to people all over the world.

Search engines

Because there were soon millions of pages of information on the Internet, finding what you wanted became slow and difficult. Search engines were invented to hunt through special

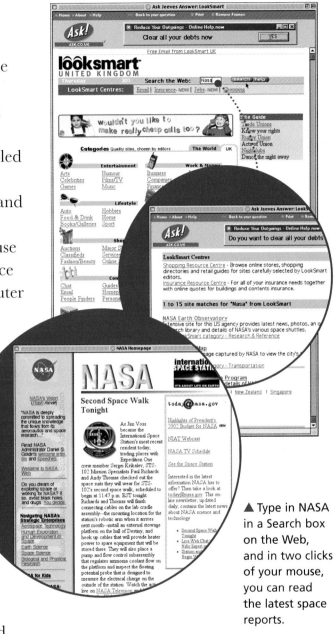

▲ Type in NASA in a Search box on the Web, and in two clicks of your mouse, you can read the latest space reports.

webpage index files, called "metafiles", and look for certain words. Now the Internet has grown even larger, there are search engines that in turn, use other search engines. With these you can find almost anything you need to know on the Internet.

What's on the Web?

The Internet has meant that people can now see more information than ever before.

You can find almost anything on the Web. As more and more people buy their own computers and start their own webpages the Web grows everyday.

▼ A Webpage under construction

Homepages

A lot of Internet companies will give people who use their company free webspace to create their own homepage. Some people use the Web to tell others about their hobbies, others use it to research their family trees or almost any other subject. The only things that limit what you put on your homepage are your imagination, and how good you are at using the **software**!

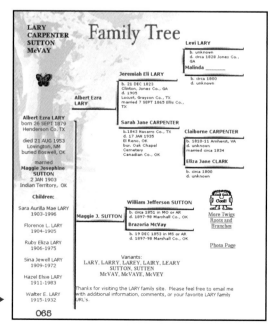

People use the Web to ▶ trace their ancestors.

Business pages

Nearly all big companies have their own homepages – some of these cost millions of pounds to write and maintain. It's important that the pages are kept up-to-date and interesting, to make sure people keep re-visiting the website. People who have a computer often go straight to the Web when they want to buy something.

▲ The Oxford University Press homepage

Online shopping

Some people buy their groceries over the Internet. If they are too busy to get to the shops they can order what they want **online** and have it delivered to their home. To save time, many people order their books and CDs from websites.

1 This person is using a website to order her family's groceries.

2 The shop gets the order and packs it up from the shelves.

4 The van delivers the groceries directly to the door.

3 A van from the supermarket drives to the house.

E-mail

Many people now use e-mail to keep in touch with their friends all over the world. You can send an e-mail much faster than you could a letter, and you can attach still pictures, movies or sound as well! It's a great way to keep in touch.

Predicting the Future

How much do you need to know?

When people first began to communicate it was just about basic things. Where was the food you needed? Where would you sleep tonight? Was it safe to move here or there?

As society became more complicated, people needed more information. Now, people are bombarded with communications all the time, and sometimes feel there is too much to cope with. How can new communications technology help us in the future? Here are four predictions. Which ones do you think will happen in the next five years?

Prediction 1

E-mail and online shopping
Computers will become more important for communication. E-mail will replace written letters. People will do all their shopping **online**, on the Internet.

Prediction 2

Computers will be fitted with information "filters" which you can program to search the Internet and present you with only the sort of information you really want to see.

Prediction 3

Homeworking
By using computers and the Internet, everyone will be able to work or study at home without having to travel to work or school at all!

Prediction 4

Instead of keyboards, computers will have notepad panels you can write on. You will also be able to use a computer just by talking to it.

Glossary

amplify Make louder.

cathode ray tube The tube which creates a television picture.

consonants Letters that start with hard sound, like the letter "t".

cuneiform Wedge-shaped symbols used for writing in ancient Babylon.

decipher Break a code so that it can be understood.

dictate Speaking whilst someone else writes down what you say.

digital radio A radio which gives better sound quality as well as other information.

engrave To cut a pattern or words into something.

hieroglyphic Picture writing.

ideograms Writing made from simple pictures of real things.

illiterate Unable to read or write.

laborious Hard work.

online Using the Internet.

papyrus Paper made from pounded reeds layered over each other.

parchment A type of paper made from very thin animal skin.

programmable You can tell a programmable machine to do specific things.

quipu Knotted string used by the Incas for communicating information about numbers.

reservoir A holder for liquid (ink).

semaphore A way of sending messages by moving large pointers or flags in different positions.

sermon A religious talk.

software Computer programs.

stylus A special pointed stick for making marks on clay when writing.

syllable A part of a word that has one sound when you say it.

taxes Money that people and companies have to pay to the government.

telegraph station A building where people send telegraph messages.

transmit Send a signal.

type Letters for printing made from lead.

vellum A type of paper made from animal skin.

vowels The five letters that make a soft sound: a, e, i, o, u.

Index

Books for further reading:

Writing by Karen Brookfield and
Invention by Lionel Bender, both published
by Dorling Kindersley

Writing by Pam Harper, published by
British Museum Press

E-mail; Internet; Computers; and World Wide Web
by Chris Ward-Johnson, published by
Cherrytree Books

How to Conquer the Internet by Ian Lewis,
published by Oxford University Press